A History of the United States Military Academy Library

Aloysius A. Norton

AVERY PUBLISHING GROUP INC.
Wayne, New Jersey

Publication of *The History of the United States Military Academy Library* is sponsored by The Friends of the West Point Library, a private, non-profit association organized in accordance with U.S.M.A. and U.S. Army regulations.

The principal function of the Friends is to help preserve West Point's literary and historic heritage, and to help the West Point Library to grow in stature as well as to enjoy the pleasures of books and book collecting. The aim of the Friends is the enrichment of the printed and manuscript collection of West Point.

Membership may be obtained by writing The Friends of the West Point Library, P.O. Box 87, West Point, New York 10996. Queries about donations, including manuscripts, documents, and graphics, should be directed to the Librarian, United States Military Academy, West Point, New York 10996.

Cover designed by Martin Hochberg
Page layout by Rudy Shur
In-house editor Jacqueline Balla

Library of Congress Cataloging-in-Publication Data

Norton, Aloysius A.
  A history of the United States Military Academy
Library.

  1. United States Military Academy. Library—History.
2. Libraries, University and college—(New York (State)—
West Point—History.   3. Military libraries—New York
(State)—West Point—History.   I. Title.
Z733.U651N67   1986   026.355′009747′31   86-7930
ISBN 0-89529-352-8

Printed in the United States of America

9 8 7 6 5 4 3 2 1

Contents

Dedicated to
my wife, Luba

Foreword

In early 1982 The Friends Of The West Point Library was formed by a group of Academy graduates, and supporters of The Military Academy, who were interested in its library and, in particular, in enhancing the development of its collection of manuscripts and rare books. At one of the early meetings the idea of The Friends sponsoring the publication of a history of the Library was suggested, but remained dormant.

We were then very fortunate that Aloysius A. Norton became affiliated with the Friends, and developed an interest in the history project which led to his authoring this work. He brought to the task unusual qualifications. A graduate of West Point who later taught English there, Norton went on to an academic career after earning his Ph.D. He has numerous publications to his credit, and is Professor Emeritus of English, U.S. Merchant Marine Academy, as well as a retired Captain, U.S. Maritime Service.

Dr. Norton relates the history of the West Point Library from its founding during the Revolutionary War (even before The Academy itself) to the present. Early library holdings were interestingly enough almost entirely written in French, reflecting the backgrounds of many of the faculty as well as the predilections of Sylvanus Thayer. After fire destroyed the old building in 1838 a new library was completed in 1841 which, with renovations, served as the West Point Library until the present edifice was opened in the autumn of 1964.

In a sense this work is more than a history of a library, it is also an intellectual history of West Point as well as the people and ideas that shaped its growth—developing, for example, the integration of the library holdings into the Military Academy teaching process.

An important part of the book is its illustrations. There are early representations of the Academy, the Library, and the Cadets themselves. Also included are Sully paintings that hang in the Library and much more.

The Friends Of The West Point Library are particularly proud that this is the first publication sponsored by them. We hope that cadets, graduates and all interested in West Point will not only find this work of interest, but that it will further stimulate their desire to utilize the great resources that this unique institution contains.

On behalf of the Friends, I want to thank Mrs. Mary G. Roebling of Trenton, New Jersey for her support of this book, the research for which was conducted by Dr. Norton at the West Point Library, with the assistance of the staff of that fine institution.

Douglas Kinnard
Brigadier General U.S. Army (Ret.)
Chairman, Friends Of The West Point Library

Preface

A library has a life of its own. It grows. It can be either neglected or nourished. It has friends—no enemies—but it can be ignored. Since it can be used over and over, it regenerates itself. A library usually has a long, long life.

The Library of the United States Military Academy has become a part of the history of the United States. Its resources first taught engineers, artillerists, and infantrymen; then geographers, astronomers, railroad builders, scientists, statesmen, and astronauts. Its place in the work of the Academy has grown, not diminished. From the most humble beginnings, it quickly became a center of French scientific learning—the greatest of its time and the faculty's source of knowledge. Over the years the Library has served a very finite purpose in supporting what was essentially a textbook education. Since World War II the Library has become an indispensable asset in a markedly diversified curriculum.

This book is one story of its life.

I wish to acknowledge the contributions of Marie Capps, Elaine Eatroff, and Susan Lintelmann to the compilation of this brief history. I also wish to thank the Librarian, Egon A. Weiss, and the Staff of the United States Military Academy Library. Finally, I'd like to thank Sharon Shelton and Joan Quinn for typing the manuscript.

The photographs are from the Archives and Special Collections Division of the Academy Library, and the West Point Museum collection.

Aloysius A. Norton, U.S.M.A., 1944
Professor Emeritus
United States Merchant Marine Academy

Introduction

A mere five hundred years ago the existence of two continents was completely unknown to the rest of the earth's people, and so their discovery was called The New World. On one of these continents, in the life spans of just three men, the United States was born, grew, and flourished. The transformation surpasses anything that has ever occurred before in the history of mankind.

To develop a wilderness into a civilization required knowledge and organization. To a large degree these attributes were derived from the early army of the United States. A few Continental leaders urged the creation of a military academy to train officers for the Engineer and Artillery forces. Their training demanded extensive study of mathematics and the other sciences. Their studies were based mainly on French models and, following their surveys of coastlines and wilderness areas, led to ordnance manufacture, construction of fortifications, canals, roads, and railroads. This army, even during the Revolutionary War, needed books to learn the military arts, which were later extended to civil engineering. These books became the nucleus of the Military Academy Library. The growth of this Library was destined by necessity, and it became a principal scientific and technical resource for the expansion of the United States up and down the east coast and westward to the Ohio and Mississippi rivers.

In the first hundred years of its existence about four thousand men graduated from the Military Academy. They were taught mainly by former graduates and learned from textbooks written from the holdings of the Academy Library. Many of these men founded other engineering schools or taught in them. The early Library played a major role in the wonder and success of the new nation.

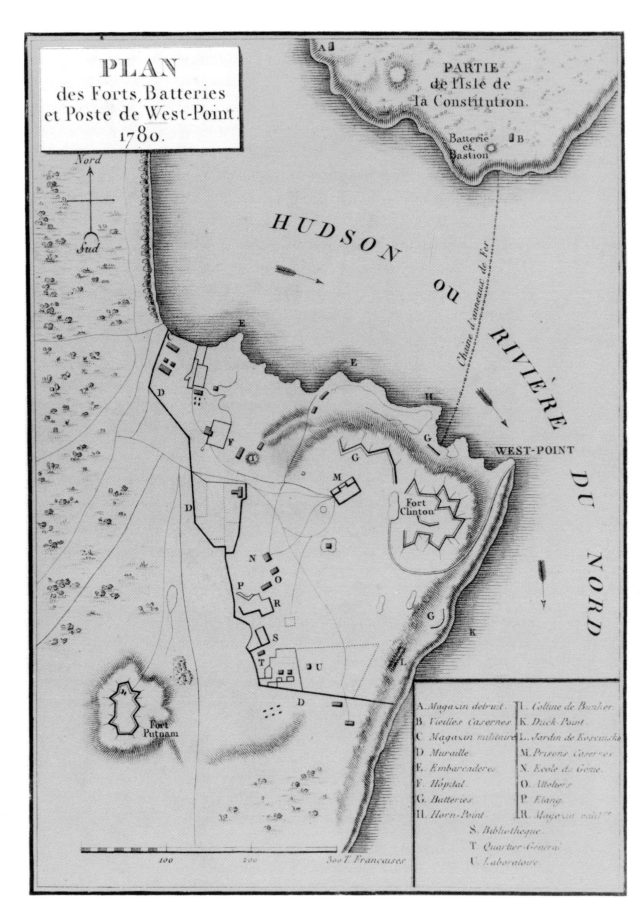

The Library is indicated by the letter S (Bibliotheque) on this map of 1780.

The Origins of the Library

Today, the United States Military Academy Library holds about one million titles in books, serials, microforms, maps, and manuscripts. By means of its computerized online information retrieval system, the Library has access to the resources of over 6,350 other libraries and can deliver bibliographies from 200 data bases. Each year, the Library sends out more books and journals on loan to other libraries than the entire contents of the Library of Colonel Thayer's time.

An exquisite map of West Point made by a French officer in 1780 clearly shows the outline of a library building and an ordnance laboratory. At the time West Point was the largest permanent garrison in the United States, occupied by a Corps of Artillerists and Engineers, and a growing number in the Corps of Invalids, drawn from Philadelphia, Massachusetts, and Connecticut. These Invalids were the honored maimed from the skirmishes and battles of the ongoing Revolutionary War, who were expected to guard stores and train young men to be officers. An assessment at the rate of one day's pay a month was levied against the officers to pay for books for the Library. This Library became the first federal library in the United States and the ancestor of today's U.S.M.A. Library.

The courses taught at West Point consisted mainly of rudimentary mathematics, and the books acquired for the Library, as ordered by Congress, were of the "most approved Authors on Tactics and the Petite Guerre." As the American Revolution ended, the Corps of Invalids dissipated. By 1784 most were gone. Margaret Corbin, the Revolutionary War heroine, was one of the few who remained. She is buried in the cemetery at West Point.

A crippling ambivalence confounded the fate of a military school. On one hand, there was a dread of standing armies, seeing them as a threat to the republican ideals of freedom and liberty, voiced mainly by Jefferson. On the other hand, there was an abhorrence of any dependence on foreigners for development

A portrait of George Washington by Gilbert Stuart given to the Library by Susan B. Warner, author and benefactor. Washington labored valiantly to establish a military academy for the new nation.

of the science of war, as expressed by Henry Knox, Washington, and Hamilton. Plans languished, and by 1785 the Army numbered less than one hundred officers and men. The construction of forts and harbor defenses was abandoned for lack of engineers to design the fortifications. Other than garrisons of twenty-five men guarding stores at Fort Pitt and fifty-five at West Point, there was no Army. However, a high regard for government property had already been established, and it can be assumed that the books at West Point were carefully guarded along with the stores.

By 1794 events following the French Revolution had sobered Congress to action. The rank of cadet, modeled on the French, was created, and the Corps of Artillerists and Engineers was increased to 250 men (mostly foreigners) and 10 officers. By degrees Congress increased the size of the Army and provided four teachers for the cadets and junior officers, who were also required to attend classes. A mysterious fire in 1796, possibly the work of a recalcitrant junior officer as arsonist, destroyed the academic building that housed books and military apparatus. Nevertheless, the cadets and junior officers continued to attend classes together, until, on March 16, 1802, Congress established a separate Corps of Engineers to conduct a Military Academy consisting of ten cadets from the Engineers and forty cadets from the Artillerists.

One of the earliest depictions of West Point, probably 1795. It is not clear which building contained the Library.

Benjamin Franklin's aversion to classical education influenced his nephew Jonathan Williams and set West Point on the path toward French scientific and mathematical studies.

The Founding of the Academy

The tradition of military academies was established in France as early as the reign of Louis XIV. Cadet companies also existed in France in 1726, 1733, and 1748. Cadet insubordination was the usual cause of school closings. In 1751 the Ecole Royale Militaire was founded. This last school furnished most of the engineers for the American Revolutionary Army. The entire process of French scientific and military education was closely observed by Benjamin Franklin during his long years in France. With Franklin for some twenty years in London and Paris was his grandnephew Jonathan Williams, destined to be the first Superintendent of the United States Military Academy. Benjamin Franklin, as much a product of the Enlightenment and New Science as any Frenchman, saw the severe limitations of traditional classical studies, Latin and Greek, as far as meeting the needs of a new nation. Change and secularization would shape the curriculum of the future. Whereas the colonial colleges followed the examples of England—Harvard (1636) after Emmanuel at Cambridge, and William and Mary (1693) after Queens at Oxford—the Military Academy would follow in the scientific and mathematical footsteps of the Ecole Militaire and the Ecole Polytechnique through the fortuitous relationship of Franklin and Williams. Williams participated with Franklin in several scientific experiments, notably his studies of the Gulf Stream and thermometrical navigation. Williams came to Jefferson's attention while Williams was serving as U.S. Commercial Agent in France. When Williams returned to the United States and took a commission in the Army, President Jefferson made him the first Superintendent at West Point.

Jonathan Williams became first Superintendent of the Academy on April 15, 1802.

Williams was eminently qualified to be chief officer of the Engineers in command of the Corps. A scientist and a scholar, Williams was active in the American Philosophical Society and was even published in its *Transactions*. Like most members of the Society, he saw the future needs of the country in science. The Royal Military Academy at Woolwich, England, provided little inspiration, compared to the French. William Newnham Bane, visiting Colonel Thayer twenty years later, would write, "A foolish prejudice has long existed in England, against the introduction of the powerful Analysis used by the French Mathematicians. Even when I was at Cambridge, many of the Old Fellows of colleges still preferred the antiquated geometrical method; though it was evident that in consequence, of pursuing it, the English were, as regarded mathematics, nearly half a century behind the disciples of La Place and La Croix."

The chief problem for the new school was a shortage of texts. Williams committed himself to the French model wherever possible. He himself lectured from his own translation of Vauban's *Fortifications*. He also appealed for a teacher of French. Francois Desire Masson was the first true teacher at the Academy. His only responsibilities were teaching French and topographical drawing. When he taught French, however, Masson lectured on engineering as well. Williams could not have found a better teacher. There were other professors, of course, but they were subject to other assignments as Engineers anywhere in the country. Subsequently, Williams was ordered to North Carolina, leaving Captains Barron and Mansfield behind. Soon Mansfield was made Surveyor-General of the Northwest Territory. Captain Barron became Acting Superintendent. Therefore, the Academy totalled one French teacher and ten cadets.

Another French-speaking addition to the staff came in 1807 when Ferdinand Hassler, a Swiss national steeped in the French system of military education, arrived at the Academy. He was a mathematician who was sorely needed to replace the absent engineering professors. Hassler brought a sizeable personal library with him from Paris; some of his books can still be seen in the Rare Book Collection of the Library. Hassler had conversed with all the prominent French scientists of his time: Lalande, Borda, Delambre, Lavoisier. His memoirs relate his visits to schools of mines in France, his studies in mineralogy and chemistry, his book-collecting in all branches of science. While at West Point, he wrote a textbook of analytic trigonometry for the use of the cadets—the first in the United States. Previously Williams had wasted no time in forming the United States Military Philosophical Society at West Point. Cadets and officers were automatically members; civilians could also join, if qualified. The Keeper of the Cabinet was in charge of the property of the Society and served as Librarian. In 1803, to add to the Library, Captain Barron bought several books of special usefulness from the private collection of Lieutenant Swift. In January of 1805 Major Wadsworth

You want for the establishment indispensably a Library, Instruments, philosophical apparatus, etc. To this I would spend the money & only the tenth part viz. 2500 to making up of the proper rooms for the Academy & rather let the Cadets lodge & board in the private houses of the place than spend the money in wood & stones.

Frederick R. Hassler, *Letter to Major Joseph G. Swift, July 26, 1812*

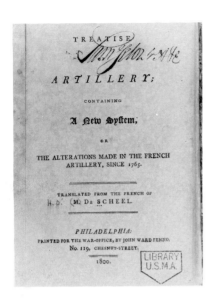

The title page of a typical work used at the Academy in its earliest years, translated from the French.

of the Engineers was allowed to purchase books for the Library, some coming by necessity from his own collection. When Colonel Williams returned in 1806, he donated thirty-four volumes and sixteen pamphlets to the Academy Library. Jared Mansfield donated a copy of his *Essays Mathematical and Physical*. Major Alexander Macomb contributed his *Treatise on Martial Law*. The Library also acquired eight manuscript volumes of General Anthony Wayne's campaigns against the Indians. In his will Benjamin Franklin left his medical, anatomical, and surgical books to Jonathan Williams, who had expressed a desire to study medicine. However, Williams was, in effect, cheated out of them by another relative. It is unlikely that any of Franklin's books came to the Academy Library through Williams. The only book with Benjamin Franklin's signature is Volume II of Belidor's *Architecture Hydraulique*, acquired between 1840 and 1853, probably as a gift. The signature has been cut out of Volume I.

Before 1812 the United States Military Philosophical Society was ostensibly more effective than the Academy itself in propagating scientific achievement. In its first years the Academy had students ranging in age from fourteen to twenty-four. Command authority for engineers, or lack of it, caused enormous dissatisfaction and even the temporary departure from the service of Colonel Williams for several years. The academic program had no true method or consistency. The Society, however, prospered and became the strongest asset of the Academy. Williams encouraged research and papers on astronomy, ordnance, meteorology, and mathematics. He held meetings in New York and Washington, attended from time to time by Thomas Jefferson, James Madison, John Quincy Adams, James Monroe, John Marshall, DeWitt Clinton, Thomas Cushing, Benjamin Latrobe, Charles Cotesworth Pinckney, Robert Fulton, Eli Whitney, and Bushrod Washington. The Society's Library at West Point owned the most up-to-date collection of scientific books in the nation. It contained the only copy of Marc Rene Montalembert's ten-volume work on fortifications and artillery in the United States. General John Armstrong gave Baron Henri Jomini's *Traite de Grand Tactique* to the Library. The Society held books by Newton, Bacon, Vignola, Marshal Saxe, and Villeneuve. In contrast to the flourishing success of the society, during 1811 and part of 1812 the Academy itself was a paper organization. On March 31, 1812, not a single instructor or cadet was in attendance.

The War of 1812 brought enormous difficulties to the Academy. There was no way to go but up. Congress reorganized the Corps of Cadets on April 29, 1812, just before the Declaration of War with Britain. This very important legislation in the history of the Academy decreed that cadets were to graduate with degrees, that they were to be organized into companies, and that summer camp was to be utilized for soldiering. Despite these ambitious and

The early Library of the Academy occupied a portion of the building at the center of this drawing of 1820.

appropriate directives, Alden Partridge, the Acting Superintendent, was sorely pressed to graduate students as soon as possible to meet the national emergency of leaderless, aimless, disorganized Militias and Army. The law authorized 250 cadets, but no definite date for uniform admission. Partridge was at odds with his faculty and controversy abounded. One solid, reliable teacher should be mentioned—Florimond Masson, the brother of Francois, now in France. Monsieur Masson kept at his work of teaching French, which was by now an absolutely necessary tool for a young engineer. Congress also authorized money for three stone buildings, completed in 1815. One became a combination lecture room, laboratory, and library.

The Thayer-McRee Book Purchase

At the close of the War of 1812 Captain Sylvanus Thayer realized the disgraceful deficiencies of the American Army. He knew that correction would come only from study of the Napoleonic military system and the progress of science in Europe. Thayer presented an appeal for furlough to the Secretary of War, James Monroe. Instead of a furlough, Thayer, together with Brevet Colonel William McRee, was ordered abroad on duty to study the European military models. Thayer was also given some five thousand dollars with which to purchase books, maps, and plans.

An extended organization of the Military Academy was proposed, and to that effect I recommended that two of our best officers be sent to Europe to examine the works of France etc., and on the Rhine and low countries, and to form a Library for the Academy.

General Joseph Gardner Swift, *Memoirs*, **1870**

Sylvanus Thayer reorganized the entire academic and disciplinary system of the Academy after he became Superintendent in 1817.

Thayer and McRee spent their year at the Ecole Polytechnique, a considerable time at the Engineering and Artillery School at Metz, and visited fortifications at Lille, Cherbourg, and Brest. Upon their return in May of 1817 newly-elected President Monroe appointed Thayer Superintendent of the Military Academy. In September the now-famous Thayer-McRee Book Purchase began to arrive from France: 1142 books, some 500 charts and maps, a variety of scientific instruments, and 257 numbers of the *Encyclopedie Methodique.* Thayer and McRee had purchased every significant book available on military science and engineering, both civil and military. They also obtained the best books on mathematics and general science. Their choices were studied and enlightened. Claudius Berard, who had come to teach French in 1815, was designated Librarian and remained so until his death in 1848. Thayer was now convinced that the French language held "the repository of military science." All cadets would now study French upon admission. To assist him, Thayer chose the French scholars Claude Crozet, who taught engineering until 1823, and Thomas Gimbrede, who taught drawing. Crozet had graduated from the Ecole Polytechnique and did postgraduate work at the School of Application for Artillerists and Engineers at Metz. He had been with Napoleon from 1809 on, through Russia, and served in the Hundred Days. Upon Partridge's removal he became Professor of Engineering. The position of Sword Master was regularly held by Frenchmen—Thomas, Trainque, Simon, Jumel, Dupare, Boulet, de Janon. Berard and his assistant of twelve years, Du Commun, taught French to the fourth-class students five days a week, from twelve to one and from two to four. The rest of the academic day was spent on mathematics. The third-class students continued their study of French as well; all could read technical French, and some could even converse. Almost all of the Thayer-McRee purchase was in French; many of the students' advanced textbooks were in French.

There was no other engineering school in the United States. Rensselaer Polytechnic Institute was founded in 1824, but did not have a Department of Engineering and Technology until 1835. They then used the Military Academy texts. Until 1850 all academic engineers came from West Point and Rensselaer. Harvard founded its Lawrence School of Engineering in 1846 with an Academy graduate as Dean and Professor of Engineering. Yale opened the Sheffield School of Engineering with an Academy graduate in the chair of Civil Engineering. The Military Academy still had the most advanced technical library in the country, almost all in French. For example, a list of seventy-nine items that Joseph G. Swift, the Chief of Engineers, ordered from England for the Academy in 1818 is far less sophisticated than those brought from France.

Most of the books in the Thayer-McRee Collection deteriorated over the years through excessive handling, humidity, and water damage. A generous gift of the U.S.M.A. Class of 1950 made possible the restoration of the Collection in 1970.

Some books in the Thayer-McRee Collection were rebound or restored. A few had to be simply boxed, as on the right.

Jared Mansfield, Professor of Natural and Experimental Philosophy (an Aristotelian term for the sciences), wrote to Thomas Jefferson on January 26, 1821, asking him to sit for a portrait by Thomas Sully. The officers and cadets of the Academy had taken up a collection of five hundred dollars for this purpose. Mansfield pointed out that paintings of George Washington and Jonathan Williams already hung in the Library. Jefferson consented, and the portrait was finished in May, four years before his death. The Library thus began its Sully collection of paintings. Sully later painted Mansfield, W. K. Armistead, J. G. Swift, A. Macomb, T. J. Leslie, C. Gratiot, James Monroe, J. J. Abert, and G. Blaney, all of which were hung in the Library.

The Thomas Sully portrait of Thomas Jefferson in the Library.

In later years the Corps acquired, as a gift from Anna Warner, a portrait of George Washington by Gilbert Stuart. Paintings by John Wesley Jarvis, G. P. Healy, and Robert W. Weir are hung in the Library at various times.

There were 250 cadets at West Point in 1822, ranging in age from fourteen to twenty-two. Those who graduated entered the Engineers, the Artillery, or the Infantry. The English gentleman, Blane, who stayed with Colonel Thayer about this time, later wrote that the students worked at their duties and studies from dawn until 9:30 p.m. He observed that they could read French as easily as English. Yet, French books were regularly translated into English when necessary for course work. For example, Captain John M. O'Connor translated Gay de Vernon's *Traite de Fortification* for his classes. Other colleges used texts translated at the Academy, and the curriculum at the Military Academy soon affected course offerings elsewhere. Henry Adams observed that West Point projected the first systematic study of science in the New World. Meanwhile, the Army numbered only six thousand men. The railroads were coming, and the Engineer graduates of the Academy would build them. There were no others.

> We are permitted to take books from the Library belonging to the Institution— The English books are generally such as are connected with military science, but the French department is miscellaneous, and embraces almost every branch of useful and entertaining literature—All the genteel families on the Point have joined in forming a reading-society which meets every Thursday evening at each house in its turn.
>
> Eliza Leslie, sister of Lt. Thomas Leslie, *Letter* to Abbey Bailey, November 25, 1823

The Library in 1822

In 1822 librarian Claudius Berard published a *Catalogue of Books* held by the Library. Curiously, the *Catalogue* contains approximately nine hundred titles, even though it would appear that there should be many more. A sampling reveals 64 books on Engineering and Fortification, 71 on Military Art and Tactics, 134 on Artillery, Infantry, Cavalry, and Military Regulations. Only a few of these are in English. Under Military Art and Tactics are James's *Military Dictionary*, Pasley's *Essay on the Military Institutions of England*, and Simon's *Treatise on Military Science*. There are further groupings under Campaigns, Architecture, Mathematics, Natural Philosophy, Geography, and History. Under Miscellaneous are Martel's *Elements of French Reading*, Johnson's *Dictionary*, Bacon's *Works*, Burke's *Works*, the *Code Napoleon*, and *Oeuvres Complètes* of Racine, Saint-Simon, Moliere, Rousseau, and Montesquieu. Librarianship was little more than bookkeeping, and even the titles in the *Catalogue* are not arranged alphabetically. Some books were undoubtedly out on permanent loan. In any event, Berard began a strict system of accounting. From 1824 on, the Library has preserved circulation records. There are no specific dates in the earliest records—just "borrowed" and "returned."

The reading time of the students was limited by both classwork and regulations. Post orders decreed that fiction and non-course books could be taken out on Saturdays and returned on Mondays;

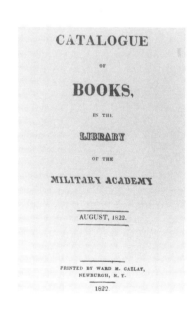

Title page of the 1822 Catalogue.

however, books used for classwork could be taken out for ten days. The Library did not have a lot to offer in the way of recreational reading. A review of the circulation records suggests some of the interests of Civil War Generals while cadets.

James E. B. Stuart read *Ancient History*, Scott's *Waverly Novels*, Prescott's *Conquest of Mexico*, Byron's *Works*, and Chateauneuf's *Grands Capitaines*; Ulysses S. Grant took out writings by Swift and Livy; Philip Sheridan was unusually infatuated by the Napoleonic era and read *Napoleon and His Marshalls*, *The Court and Camp of Bonaparte*, *Memoirs of Josephine*, and *Napoleon in Exile*, as well as *Demosthenes* and *The Life and Writings of Samuel Johnson*; Thomas J. Jackson read *Cavalry Tactics*, Turner's *Chemistry*, and Duane's *Military Dictionary*; George B. McClellan enjoyed such histories as *Queen Elizabeth*, *The Court and Camp of Bonaparte*, *Charlemagne*, *Memoirs of Picton*, Alexander's *Wellington*, and *History of the Jews*. Robert E. Lee studied Montholon's *Memoirs of Napoleon*. Clearly, the favorites were books about Napoleon and novels by Scott and Cooper. Records also reveal that Ambrose E. Burnside, a great practical joker, never took out a book. Perhaps he was content with reading some of the periodicals to which the Library subscribed, such as the *North American Review*, the *Edinburgh Review*, *Niles Weekly Register*, the *American Quarterly Review* or, if he was homesick, *The American Farmer*.

There is a fine library connected with the Academy from which cadets can get books to read in their quarters. I devoted more time to these than to books relating to the course of studies. Much of the time, I am sorry to say, was devoted to novels, but not those of a trashy sort.

Ulysses S. Grant,
***Personal Memoirs*, 1885**

The Rise of Civil Engineering

From 1816 on, under the direction of the immigrant French engineer Simon Bernard, the Board of Engineers for Fortifications evolved into the Board of Engineers for Internal Improvement, consisting of its Chief Engineer Joseph Totten, a civilian engineer, and twenty Army officers. These men immediately began internal improvement works on all the early canals, and began construction of the Baltimore and Ohio Railroad. Andrew Jackson's administration took exception to this federal assistance, and the projects were severed with the elimination of the Board. This action resulted in wholesale resignations from the Army. Civil engineers were desperately needed for the flush of railroad construction. The Board of Visitors to West Point in 1829 actually encouraged the new ascendancy of civil engineering in the curriculum at the Academy, whose Library had the largest technical and engineering collection in the country: 692 volumes on engineering, of which 308 were on civil engineering—tunneling, railroad building, roads, bridges, and grading. Also in 1829, twenty-four cadets formed a society called the American Association for the Promotion of Science, Literature, and the Arts. Associate Societies were soon started at other schools of higher education. From these various, loosely-connected societies came the American Association for the Advancement of Science. The members of the Class of 1832 were intensely supportive of civil engineer knowledge, and were given special library privileges of two hours a day. The Library was often consulted by graduates, and it seems that many graduates on projects borrowed books that were sent to them. Sometimes books were lost in transit. The map-making of the western lands from 1820 was done largely by the Army Topographical Engineers. By 1870 they had charted nine-tenths of the West. They also completed international boundary surveys, surveys of the Great Lakes, various coast surveys, and geodetic surveys. The reputations of the graduates as builders of railroads and canals expanded. William G. McNeill planned the Chesapeake and Ohio Canal; in 1842 George W. Whistler became Consulting Engineer to the Russian government and directed the building of the Moscow-St. Petersburg Railroad. Graduates also designed the first railroads in Mexico and Cuba.

Another *Catalog of the Library*, printed in 1830 by J. Desnoues, includes a listing of 2,852 books. Most of the Military Art books are in French, London publications being about ten percent. Civil Engineering has a complete set of Palladio's works in French, Semple's *Treatise on Building in Water*, Tredgold's *Practical Treatise on Rail Roads and Carriages*, and Mrs. Margaret Bryan's *Lectures on Natural Philosophy* and her *Compendious System of Astronomy*. Either the *Catalog* was incomplete or there was a prodigious increase by 1834, because the American State Papers on Military Affairs report more than eight thousand books in the Library in June of 1834. On November 12, 1838, Major Delafield reported the ordering of a $4,800 book purchase from Paris, and a $2,500 book purchase from London. On March 27, 1839, he wrote to Mr. J. C. White, a New York purchasing agent, requesting faster delivery. He asked White not to wait until all the books had arrived, and was irked because other libraries had already received some of the items. His order of seventy copies of Bayar's *Dictionary,*

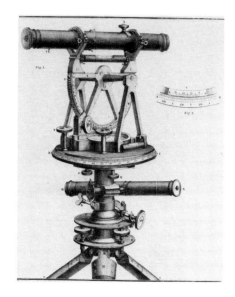

Drawing of a theodolite by Cadet Meriwether Lewis Clark for the 1830 edition of *Elements of Surveying* by Professor of Mathematics Charles Davies. The theodolite was used to survey the western lands of the United States.

In 1838 a fire destroyed the Library. The books were housed in the West Point Hotel for three years.

French and English on May 7, 1839, indicates that the study of French had not diminished. The Library still had a preponderance of works in French. An indication of the amount spent on the books can be realized by the fact that, at this time, a second lieutenant earned $760 a year, and a colonel, $2,450. A chief engineer on a railroad project earned about $6,000.

On March 5, 1838, a fire destroyed the Academy building that housed academic departments and the Library. Unlike the fire of 1796 the damage to the contents of the Library was far less. Cadets rushed into the building and managed to throw most of the books and paintings out the windows into the snow. Many books were damaged; some were lost. All in all, the loss was tolerable—replacements were purchased and remaining books were repaired and rebound. Surviving volumes were moved to the Hotel Dining Room, where they remained for three years.

The Library Building of 1841

Major Delafield had placed a model of his toy, the library, on top of the woodhouse. It was very convenient for us and in it we stored the cartridges which we managed to accumulate.

Whitman Bailey, "Childhood Recollections," *News of the Highlands,* July 4, 1903

Major Richard Delafield, Superintendent, wasted no time in designing a new library. Various plans were submitted, but the final design—his own—was an Elizabethan Gothic design, which set the style for futre buildings at the Academy, such as old Central Barracks. Congress constantly delayed allocating money for the building of the Library; when it was approved, the amount was too low for any contractor. Therefore, using enlisted men and local journeymen, Superintendent Delafield built a stone structure, 160 feet wide and 78 feet in depth, castellated and corniced with red sandstone, at a total cost of $50,216.86. The building served several purposes. The Library was located in the East Wing, thirty-one feet high, forty-six feet square. The first floor of the West Wing provided offices for the Superintendent and the Adjutant, the Quartermaster, and the Treasurer of the Academy. The lecture hall and apparatus of the Philosophical Department were located above them.

The building, which also housed a contemporary astronomical laboratory, had huge cement columns that supported an equatorial telescope built by Henry Fitz of New York for five thousand dollars. It was placed in a circular dome, twenty-seven feet in diameter, just in time for Professor Bartlett's exciting observations of the comet in 1843. He is also said to be the first in the United States to use photographic equipment in conjunction with observations and measurements. A transit instrument, made by Merz and Mahler in Munich for eleven hundred dollars, was placed in the northeast tower; a mural circle by Troughton and Simms of London occupied the northwest tower.

During the construction of the Library a reconstruction of sorts was taking place at the Academy. The Regulations of 1839 removed the permanent tenure of the Superintendent. Slowly and inevitably the permanent professors of the various Departments celebrated their autonomy by becoming a power unto themselves at the Academy. Rivalry for class hours intensified, and each professor depended on the strength of his own character and his tenacity to establish the importance of his discipline. Such rivalry could hardly have been beneficial to the Library. An academic board of strong-willed professors could hold off the best reform gambits of most superintendents. In 1866 superintendents at the Military Academy were no longer drawn solely from the Corps of Engineers. In 1877 Superintendent J. M. Schofield and Chief of the Army W. T. Sherman attempted to remove tenure from the heads of the departments by installing young officers. They failed.

Andre Freis enlisted in the Army on May 1, 1841. On November 5, 1844, Private Freis was assigned to duty in the Library under the supervision of Claudius Berard, still the Librarian. Freis worked in the Library for fifty years, until his death on March 8, 1899. Learning as he worked, by 1871 Freis had become such a competent assistant librarian that Congress gave him a thousand dollars a year compensation in addition to his pay and allowances. Like most Alsace immigrants, Freis spoke English, French, and German. He had refused to re-enlist in 1851 unless he was given ten dollars a month extra pay. The Superintendent, Captain Henry Brewerton, wrote to Brigadier General Joseph G. Totten, Chief of Engineers, and threatened to close the Library if Private Freis did not get his supplementary pay to justify his long hours of duty. Superintendent Bernard took up the continuing battle for extra compensation—every re-enlistment time—by once writing, "The sum of $1,000 a year is not more than many private professional gentlemen, who make no pretensions to large or general libraries, expend in keeping themselves with recent works on some single science or branch of knowledge."

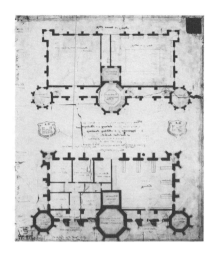

The plan of the 1841 Library completed by Major Richard Delafield and dated December 12, 1839.

An early representation of the 1841 Library clearly shows the astronomical laboratory mounted in the towers.

The 1841 Library with the telescope housing in the center.

The rear of the 1841 Library with the telescope mount clearly visible.

The Lean Years of
the Mexican War

Be that as it may, one thousand dollars a year was the usual expenditure that Congress allowed for the purchase of books from 1838 to 1852. Acquisitions were stubbornly erratic; as few as fifty volumes were added to the Library in 1844, and as many as seven hundred in 1850. No appropriations whatever were designated for books in 1846, 1847, or 1848. These years of the Mexican War may have been difficult for the Library, but the exploits of the graduates in the war secured the reputation of the Academy in the Army, in Congress, and throughout the nation. In 1853 librarian Henry Coppee recorded that there was "no permanent fund for the increase of the Library." Donations from other colleges, graduates, and friends, plus the exchange of duplicates with other institutions, did help. Annual borrowing amounted to twelve thousand books being circulated, at least three-quarters of them borrowed by the faculty.

Church groups were also generous in their donations of books during these lean years. The faculty included eleven successive chaplains who served as Professors of the Department of Geography, History, and Ethics between 1813 and 1896. Superintendent Delafield required chapel attendance of officers and professors on Sunday, as did his successor, Superintendent Brewerton. Absences had to be justified in writing. Such interest in religion led to the acquisition of religious and inspirational books, and growing interest in the Old Testament and the Jews. The catalogue of this period lists *Josephus, The Genuine Works of the learned and Authentic Jewish Historian and Celebrated Warrior;* M. Mayer, *The History of the Jews*; Thomas B. D. Godwin, *Moses and Aaron and Ecclesiastical Sites Used by the Ancient Hebrews*; David Jennings, *Jewish Antiquities*; and H. H. Mitman, *History of the Jews*.

Henry Coppee presided over an inventory of 16,036 books and 300 maps and charts. Another report, that of January 10, 1853, states that there were 15,500 volumes in the library. Apparently titles were sometimes counted with all volumes of a set included as one item; at other times, inventory figures were arrived at by other methods. Coppee remained Librarian for six years. He later published two fine pocket manuals of enormous practicality for Civil War officers. One, *The Field Manual for Battalion Drill*, was translated and adapted from the French in 1862; the other, *Field Manual of Courts-Martial*, was published in 1863. Each book was innovatively organized and could easily be carried in a shirt pocket. The Library still has copies. Interestingly, the Library at this time contained many engineering books published by Military Academy graduates such as D. H. Mahan, H. W. Halleck, and J. G. Totten. The United States was beginning to catch up to the French. Coppee was the last of the Librarians to take his library

Henry Coppee, Librarian from October 1, 1851 to May 1, 1855.

Absalom Baird was Librarian from May 1, 1855 to August 31, 1859. He had an extensive battle record and served in the Freedmen's Bureau.

Whistler studied drawing under Robert W. Weir at West Point and delighted in drawing these trim, elongated cadets. Several examples of his work hang in the West Point Room of the Library.

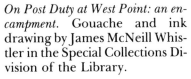

On Post Duty at West Point: an encampment. Gouache and ink drawing by James McNeill Whistler in the Special Collections Division of the Library.

work seriously for some time. His background shaped him into a true scholar. A man of prominent French ancestry, he attended Yale College and worked as a Civil Engineer, learning on the job, before coming to West Point. He graduated in 1841 and returned to teach French in 1848. Soon after, he joined the Department of Geography, History, and Ethics. After leaving the Army, he became the first President of Lehigh University and later a Regent of the Smithsonian. He has an impressive list of published works. Absalom Baird of the Mathematics Department succeeded him for four years.

A Variety of Librarians

Oliver Otis Howard, Librarian from August 31, 1859 to June 21, 1860, and later Superintendent in 1881 and 1882.

One of the Academy's most outstanding graduates of almost incredible achievement was delighted to be Librarian because, as he wrote to his mother on September 24, 1859, "[I] am Librarian, which gives me ten dollars per month more pay." Oliver Otis Howard entered Bowdoin College at the age of sixteen. After graduation he entered the Military Academy and graduated fourth in a class of forty-six in 1854. In 1857 he joined the faculty to teach mathematics, but soon departed for the Civil War, participating in battles from Bull Run to Gettysburg. He lost his right arm early in the war at Fair Oaks, during the Peninsular Campaign of 1862. Returning to duty, he fought from Atlanta to the Carolinas. On May 12, 1865, Howard was appointed Commissioner of the Bureau of Refugees, Freedmen, and Abandoned Lands. Hampton Institute, Howard, Straight, Atlanta, and Fisk Universities were founded under his direction. Later, as Special Indian Commissioner during the Indian Wars in the West, he persuaded Cochise of the Chiricahua Apaches to surrender in 1872. He also persuaded Chief Joseph of the Nez Perces to surrender at Bear Paws Mountains, Montana, in 1877, and finally defeated the Bannocks and Piutes. Howard became Superintendent of the Academy in December of 1880 and served until 1882. During his tenure, Mark Twain was a frequent visitor to West Point and lectured to the Cadets.

John C. Kelton served as Librarian for a short period in 1861. His interests were undoubtedly elsewhere, as were those of Howard before him and Herman Biggs after him. Kelton came to the Academy at the age of nineteen and graduated in 1851. In 1857 he returned as an assistant instructor of tactics and established a creditable military gymnastics program at the Academy. In 1859 he took a leave of absence and journeyed to Europe. Upon his return, he published a *Manual of Bayonet*. Kelton also published a definitive *Pigeons as Couriers in the Military Service* in 1882. He ended his career as Adjutant-General of the Army, a position in

John Cunningham Kelton, Librarian from June 21, 1860 to April 24, 1861.

A rear view of the Library during the Civil War, before the building of the railroad under the Plain ruined the astronomical laboratory.

which he made many reforms. Biggs, the Assistant Quartermaster at the Academy, probably became Librarian by default as a result of the war drain. The Library, for all intents and purposes, remained in the able hands of Andre Freis.

A *Supplement to the Catalogue* of the Library was published in 1859. The listings are still short in the area of the humanities, such as moral philosophy, poetry, religion, and history. Notable additions include novels by William Makepeace Thackeray and W. Gilmore, but technical and scientific publications overwhelmingly dominate. Someone with a sense of humor acquired item 8013: Adler, G. J., *Letters of a Lunatic, or, a brief Exposition of my*

University Life, during the years of 1853-54. Cadets were expected to obtain their educations in the classrooms and from the textbooks. There was neither time nor necessity for dabbling in the contents of the Library. Recreational reading was also a luxury, and most educators of the era thought it was a waste of time that would lead to a softening of the brain. Special books were used by cadets of the two debating societies, the Dialectic and the Amosophic, who maintained their own small, separate collections. Quite appropriately in 1860 the Congressional Military Committee (chaired by Secretary of War Jefferson Davis) found the Library deficient in historical works, literary reviews, and magazines. In his highly detailed *Diary* of his Civil War days as a cadet, Paul Dahlgren (son of Admiral John Dahlgren) wrote that he visited the Library almost daily to follow the progress of the war in the newspapers, which arrived by river boat. He was especially eager to learn of his father and his fleet establishing communication with Sherman, and the taking of Savannah. Dahlgren also found time to take out novels by Melville and Cooper and to read Longfellow and *Harper's Magazine*. Further evidence that some cadets did have the time to read came to light with a fire in a cadet barracks in February of 1871. A list of burned books includes five of Cooper's novels, three issues of *Harper's Magazine*, Lockhart's *History of Napoleon Bonaparte* (Volume I), and Lamont's *Seasons with the Sea Horses*. All were replaced.

Nevertheless, the deficiencies of the Library were recognized by Superintendent T. G. Pitcher, who wrote:

Herman Biggs had a short tenure as Librarian from April 24, 1861 to October 9, 1861.

> Our Library does not keep pace with the progress of improvement at the Institution, and with the very limited appropriation, and the high price of Books, it is not possible to make it do so. It does not compare favorably in *Extent* with the 3rd Class Colleges in the Country, and will not admit of comparison with those belonging to the 1st and 2nd Classes, except in one or two professional specialties.
>
> We are, year after year, told that we are deficient at West Point in *literary* attainment, a natural result of course, arising from our overcrowded scientific course of study—and it is believed that a considerable addition of literary matter to our Library will to a great extent remedy this defect.

His solution to the problem was of staggering originality. Just as the Library of Congress received copies of every copyrighted book published in the United States, the Academy should do the same (with the exception of fiction). Had this plan been adopted by Congress, it would have been necessary for the Academy to build a huge new library instead of a riding hall in 1905.

Mr. Freis, good old man—was he ever young?—was always ready to aid me. Though I was one of a group of romping boys who disturbed his serenity by unseemly noise playing "I spy!" around the building, he never laid it against me or others. He must have perceived that the architect had designed the building with sole reference to that exhilarating game. Why else were all those buttresses constructed?

William Whitman Bailey, "Childhood Recollections," *News of the Highlands*, July 4, 1903

The End of French Supremacy

Stephen V. Benet, Librarian from October 9, 1861 to January 16, 1864.

No nation or its institutions are ever the same after a long, serious war. The Civil War marked the end of French supremacy at West Point. An April 20, 1877 report reads, "The French language was formerly indispensable for the reason that a large part of the scientific text-books used at the Academy were printed in that language. Now they are all in English and hence French, though still important, is no logner indispensable." French was retained largely for use in diplomacy and as the universal language of travelers. The French defeats of 1870 and 1871 completed the decline of the French military reputation. Spanish had already found its way into the curriculum as a sequel to the Mexican War.

During these years the Librarians included men of various achievements but, more often, of more significant successes later in their careers. During the Civil War Stephen Vincent Benet acted as Librarian; however, his principal duties were in experimenting with Parrot Guns at the West Point Foundry in Cold Springs. He found time to publish a *Treatise on Military Law and the Practice of Courts-Martial* and to translate Baron Henri Jomini's *The Political and Military History of the Campaign of Waterloo* in 1862. He later became Chief of Ordnance. Edward Carlisle Boynton, the succeeding Librarian, earned his scholarly fame with the *History of West Point, and its Military Importance during the American Revolution*, first published in 1863. After Boynton, Robert Henry Hall served as Librarian while Aide-de-Camp to Superintendent Schofield. Hall labored for years in compiling *Laws of Congress Relative to West Point and the United States Military Academy from 1786 to 1877* with several supplements. He patiently traced and published a *List of Cadets Admitted to the United States Military Academy from its Establishment till September 30, 1876.*

Edward Carlisle Boynton, Librarian from January 1, 1864 to September 1, 1871. He is shown here with his family at the rear of the Library.

(upper left) Robert Henry Hall, Librarian from September 1, 1871 to November 1, 1878.

(upper right) Edgar Wales Bass, Librarian from November 1, 1878 to July 1, 1881.

(left) Charles Erskine Scott Wood, Librarian from July 1, 1881 to August 30, 1882.

Chaplain William Morton Postlethwaite, Professor of Geography, History, and Ethics. Librarian from September 7, 1882 to January 22, 1885.

George Breckenridge Davis, Librarian from January 22, 1885 to August 28, 1888.

The next Librarian, Edgar Wales Bass, returned to West Point the year following his graduation to teach mathematics; his duties as Librarian lasted from 1878 to 1881. Bass eventually became one of the foremost mathematicians in the country by developing more efficient methods of teaching trigonometry and differential calculus than those before him, who had used imperfect definitions. His textbooks were used across the country. His successor, Charles Erskine Scott Wood, wrote many volumes of poetry: *A Masque of Love, The Poet In The Desert*, and *Sonnets to Sappho*. He was a special friend of Mark Twain and arranged for the printing of *Date, 1601*. Wood was followed by William M. Postlethwaite, one of those eleven who served as chaplains and as professors of geography, history, and ethics. After his death the succeeding chaplains no longer headed an academic department. Chaplain Postlethwaite, it appears, was the first civilian Librarian since Berard. A fine historian, George Breckenridge Davis, was Librarian for only a year and a half. Davis published Civil War histories and studies of constitutional, international, and military law. None of these men made any traceable marks on the Library. Their work was a part-time responsibility, for which the Librarian was paid one hundred and twenty dollars a year in additional pay. And, Andre Freis was still doing his job.

To indicate the modest parameters of the Library's budget, the Report of October 12, 1881, tells of a "monthly charge of two cents and five mills made against each cadet for the use of the *Webster's Unabridged Dictionary.*" The money collected was more than enough to pay for the dictionary; the surplus was used to pay for damages to books. At this date there was $200.73 in the fund. On June 1, 1881, the Library could claim 28,208 volumes, and 2,338 unbound pamphlets. These numbers represented an increase over the previous year of 458 books and 132 pamphlets. The following years found little change in the rate of acquisition. An order published in 1883 allowed cadets to take books out of the Library for one week. This policy was a startling new innovation, since previously they could read them only in the Library.

Renovation of the Library

The West Shore Railroad began its tunneling under the Plain in 1881. The trains began running in 1883. As soon as it became apparent that the vibrations of the construction and the trains would distort the readings of the astronomical instruments mounted above the Library, the railroad arranged for the construction of a modern astronomical observatory near Lusk Reservoir. The Library could now plan to expand into the space about

to be vacated. The space previously occupied by the administrative offices had been usurped by the Department of Natural and Experimental Philosophy in 1871. The Library, still in its original section of the building, was already crowded. By 1891 it contained 36,000 volumes. The East Academic Building was under construction. A plan was developed to move all classes and offices for instruction out of the Library building, remove the stone piers supporting the old astronomcial laboratory, and renovate the entire building.

By September of 1893 there were 318 cadets at the Academy, 36,062 books in the Library, and no approval for renovation. Books were piled on desks and tables, on the floor, and in the corners. It was nearly impossible to find anything. Things were further complicated by the death of Andre Freis, the Assistant Librarian. His death amplified the confusion because he was the only person who knew the contents of the Library and the approximate location of specific items. It took only a short time to appreciate the great loss brought about by his death. The Association of Graduates solicited donations for a monument to Freis. Contractor William McMelkin of Newburgh erected a stone monument in his memory bearing the inscription, "This stone was erected by the graduates of the Military Academy as a memorial of Andre Freis, born 1820, died 1894, who as Assistant Librarian, served this school faithfully for fifty years." The name Andre Freis was inscribed on the opposite face. The monument was placed near the old entrance to the cemetery under a chestnut tree. The nine-foot, rough-cut stone still stands, although the inscription is no longer legible.

Andre Freis was Assistant Librarian from 1844 to 1894.

Peter Smith Michie, Librarian from August 28, 1888 to February 16, 1901.

At long last on January 16, 1895, Congress permitted plans, specifications, and estimates for renovation to be submitted. The interior cement columns were to be removed, the old observatory wing altered, fireproofing installed, and new cases purchased. A modern library was the goal. First, R. M. Hunt and then his son, R. H. Hunt, designed the interior. The estimate for renovation came to $63,100. Another $6,900 was added for books and related equipment, to total $70,000. As Librarian, Peter Smith Michie suffered most of the travail during these difficult years. Michie, Professor of Natural and Experimental Philosophy, was the author of *Elements of Analytical Mechanics*, which went through many editions, a biography, and *Practical Astronomy*. His Assistant Librarian, Dr. Otto Plate, who had taken the place of Andre Freis, would hold things together after the unexpected death of Michie in February of 1902. Once again contractors would not do the work for the amount allocated by Congress. As a result, one of the world's foremost engineers and builder of the Panama Canal, George W. Goethals, on duty as the Instructor of Practical Military Engineering and in command of a company of engineers at the

The Library was renovated under the supervision of George W. Goethals, who removed the astronomical devices at the tops of the towers. The Old Chapel in the foreground was later moved to the cemetery, where it now stands.

A view of the interior of the 1841 Library after its renovation.

Another view of the interior of the Library after the renovation of 1901.

Samuel Escue Tillman, Librarian from February 16, 1901 to July 1, 1902.

Academy, supervised the renovation. By September 24, 1901, the Superintendent could report that a commodious and excellent library for the spread of military knowledge was complete. By now, it was utterly obvious that Professor S. E. Tillman, interim Librarian, could not reassemble the Library and remain head of the Department of Chemistry, Mineralogy, and Geology. A billet for Librarian was needed, and a somewhat larger appropriation than usual, to supply the necessary military literature. The mission of the Library had come a long way from that of its French engineering days. After one hundred years, the Superintendent's Report stated, "The Library should present the actual state of knowledge in all branches at the Military Academy and in the related branches. The whole profession of the soldier should be covered by its books, and it should offer every facility to cadets for general culture by reading." Librarian S. E. Tillman's Report for the year ending June 30, 1902, consists of some fifteen lines and lists only the number of books in the Library and notice of the completion of the project to provide more space. The Library had 46,711 books and 8,028 pamphlets.

The Arrival of Edward S. Holden

Edward Singleton Holden, Librarian from July 1, 1902 to March 16, 1914.

One of the most significant events in the history of the Library occurred upon the resignation of Dr. Otto Plate, who returned to his native Strassburg after eight years as Assistant Librarian. Dr. Edward S. Holden, an Academy graduate, assumed the position vacated by Plate on a temporary basis. Holden's main task was to assist in the publications associated with the Centennial Anniversary of the Military Academy. Holden, as it turned out, was ideally suited to bring the Library into the twentieth century. A man of broad interests, he had been President of the University of California, a Director of the Lick Observatory for ten years, and Director of the Washburn Observatory in Madison, Wisconsin. He also had considerable library experience. Tillman's report for the year ending June 30, 1902, undoubtedly written by Holden, has five pages of small print, as contrasted with the fifteen lines of the previous year. The report credits the Assistant Librarian with remarkable changes in the Library's operations. The card catalogue, previously arranged in an elementary system of author and subject, was enlarged considerably to include subtitles and subjects. Holden personally supervised a number of officers on the staff at the Academy in accomplishing this onerous task, beginning first with the military works and later the important technical and professional works. Some titles had ten or thirty cards where they previously had two. Holden also instituted a more efficient system for the classification of military books, and inspired faculty members to begin the indexing of various military journals and branch journals. Professional bibliographical articles were prepared, and systematic battle references listed with their sources. A card catalogue of the writings of Academy graduates was started, as well as a list of portraits of graduates, wherever they might be found in library books. The holdings of the department libraries were integrated into the main library catalogue. In addition, the first serious, systematic collection of manuscripts pertaining to all the present and past regiments of the Army of the Revolution and the Civil War was begun. Finally, the current status of the military schools of foreign countries was accumulated through the Bureau of Military Information, Adjutant-General's Office.

This surge of activity was supplemented by rearranging the physical facilities of the Library for easy usage and as an attraction for cadets coming to inspect the newly-installed bulletin boards and maps of contemporary interest. Holden also purged the Library of outdated or duplicate editions, opened a Post Library for enlisted men with some of the excess, and sent the pertineent remainder off to the Artillery School or back to the Government Printing Office.

Holden was not stiffly serious in his efforts. He arranged with the Book Lovers' Library of Philadelphia to keep 125 of their new books on the Academy Library shelves on a lease basis. This innovation would provide light reading, yet not commit unnecessary expenditure for their purchase or space for their permanent retention. In the same spirit of conservation and economy he arranged for the loan of two portraits of George Washington by Gilbert Stuart to the Library, and a considerable number of valuable gifts and books. For the first time since Thayer's voyage and purchases of 1815, an aggressive program of acquisition commenced.

It should come as no surprise that on July 27, 1902, the Secretary of War appointed Holden as Librarian under the aegis of a bill by Congress designating the position of Librarian at the Academy. In his first Report of the Librarian, Holden pointed out that one Librarian and four enlisted men, one a janitor as well, could not adequately serve the Library's needs. There were 81 officers, 446 cadets, 20 enlisted men, and 35 civilians with library privileges. The Library was accumulating about 5,000 items a year and subscribed to 142 periodicals. Cadets were drawing about 750 books a month from the Library—some, of course, over and over in the instance of fiction. Holden gave regular lectures to each fourth class, arranged special exhibits, established permanent exhibits, and enlarged the collection of manuscripts. His special attention was given to making bibliographies of West Point, the Academy, and the graduates. He also instituted the Dewey system of classification and continued the burdensome task of reclassifying all the books in the Library.

Plutarch's *Lives, The Virginians, Faust,* the *Thoughts of the Emperor Marcus Aurelius* and a hundred other great books of past centuries have far more to do with present realities than most of the articles in most of the magazines; and this is true in the strictest sense. The general principles of life are taught in the world's great books. In the long run success will come to a life founded on general principles, and will be withheld from lives founded upon temporary expedients.

Edward S. Holden,
Address to Third Class,
September 12, 1903

Anna B. Warner by Orlando Campbell. Miss Warner arranged, with the cooperation of Mrs. Russell Sage, for West Point to acquire Constitution Island, her home and estate, upon her death in 1915. A prominent author, she published *West Point Colors* in 1903. She is buried in the West Point Cemetery.

Needless to say, a marked increase in the use of the Library followed. In September of 1904 the Library began night hours, weekdays until 9:30 p.m. The users grew to 96 officers, 462 cadets, 19 enlisted men, and 95 civilians. An incredible 26,000 books were added to the Library between 1901 and 1909. By 1913 the total number of books would be 90,000. There were some 300,000 cards in the catalogue. The Library had truly been modernized. Harvard University was spending twenty-eight dollars per student annually to provide for its libraries; the Academy was now up to twenty-three dollars per cadet for a Corps of 574. The only significant setback was the death of Sergeant James Maher on January 20, 1908. He had been Assistant Librarian for fourteen years.

Holden had many plans for the Library that were never realized because of a shortage of money or manpower. His staff consisted of Sergeant Maher, and Privates Cody, Collins, Swett, and Brownley. When Maher died, a civilian, Mr. Ostrander, became Assistant Librarian. The Library now subscribed to 180 newspapers and periodicals, about one-third of them from Europe and South America. Holden consistenlty appealed for gifts from graduates and civilian donors. He anticipated today's audio-visual techniques in seeking appropriations year after year for his "Instruction through the Eye" exhibits, but had no apparent success in establishing this program. He also did the tedious work of designing a Dewey Decimal system for the Military History section, a masterful achievement. The *Library Bulletin* of April, 1914, No. 19, announced his death. It states, "Dr. Holden realized the needs of the Library for years to come and made due provisions for them, so that it will be but a matter of routine to carry out the plans he has formulated." A few paragraphs later it states, "It was always a matter of regret to Dr. Holden that the valuable collections of the Library were not more freely used. . . ." To this day the Library has treasures that remain unseen.

The Library During the World Wars

The *Library Bulletin* of April, 1914, states that James E. Runcie left a fourteen-year law practice in Havana to assume the duties of Librarian. Major Runcie realized that the character of the Library had been firmly fixed by Dr. Holden, and he thought that it should remain unchanged. In his words, the Library "consisted primarily of military works, including military history and the history of the art and science of war; a collection of general literature and history such as is indispensable for every institution giving education of a general character; a collection of public

James E. Runcie, Librarian from March 16, 1914 to October 31, 1919.

documents issued by the federal government and the governments of the several states and some municipalities; and special collections bearing on the studies which are characteristic of the course of instruction at the Academy." As World War I progressed, Runcie began collecting current literature on the ensuing war, but he believed that most of it would prove ephemeral. By the end of World War I the Library had exceeded 100,000 volumes.

There is no mention of the Library in the various Superintendent's Reports from 1918 through 1924. Margery Bedinger was the Librarian from 1921 to 1926. Apparently, she was not pleased with her experience, because in 1930 she attacked the Academy, its staff, the mental condition of the cadets, and library practices in the *New Republic*. Oscar Woolverton Griswold's response was published a few months later in the *National Republic*. The Library must have been doing something right: the first Rhodes Scholarships were awarded to two members of the class of 1925 and to one member of the class of 1923. For twenty-one years the War Department had refused to permit applications to be submitted by cadets or graduates on active duty. The policy change permitted one cadet and one officer to apply each year. Another landmark of no particular scholarly attainment was the making of *Classmates* in 1924 by Inspiration Pictures, Inc.—the first full-length feature film at the Academy.

A policy was developed at this time, leading to the appointment of disabled, retired graduates as Librarians. The policy echoed somewhat the role of the Invalids in the earliest days of the Library. Edward Aloysius Everts lasted only a year and a half as Librarian. He had a natural lifetime interest in books and learning, but had a frail constitution and could not hold the position for long. His successor, Elbert Eli Farman, held the title from 1928 to 1942. Farman witnessed the growth of the Corps to 1,960 and then, in June of 1942, to 2,496 cadets. The circulation figures rose dramatically from 29,601 to 41,796 with the increase in enrollment. When William Jackson Morton assumed the duties of Librarian in 1944, there were 120,338 books. The demands on the Library increased dramatically with the war. An enormous number and variety of inquiries all but overwhelmed the Library staff. An enlisted soldier Archivist was assigned to the Library. During Farman's tenure the Library began to employ qualified civilian library personnel. This trend toward real professional librarianship was quite gradual; it took considerable time to eliminate the dependency of the Library staff on enlisted men. The Superintendent's Report of 1945 states that getting cadets to read good books has always been a problem; nevertheless, the Academy took pride in reporting a victory over the Navy. During the preceding academic year the average number of books read was 8 per cadet; at Annapolis it was only 4.7 per midshipman.

Margery Bedinger, Librarian from March 21, 1921 to July 22, 1926.

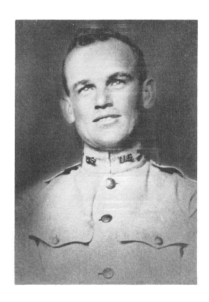

Edward Aloysius Everts, Librarian from January 20, 1927 to June 30, 1928.

Elbert Eli Farman, Jr., Librarian
from 1928 to 1942.

William Jackson Morton, Jr.,
Librarian from 1943 to 1957.

The 1841 Library as it appeared 100 years later, during World War II.

The Professional Growth
of the Library

At the end of World War II every effort was made to collect histories of combat units, often privately printed or printed abroad. Officers of combat units, many of whom were not graduates, were most generous in adding to the Academy's collections. The New York Historical Society and the National Archives began gift programs of microfilms of orderly books and correspondence important to the history of the Academy. In February of 1946 the designation of civilian Archivist was given to Sidney Forman, who had done the work since 1943 as a corporal in the Army. The Thayer Collection began being assembled in one place in the Library from the various shelves throughout the stacks. A year later Hobart College Library presented a collection of military works that had belonged to Brigadier General Joseph G. Swift, the first graduate. The collection indicated not only his personal interests, but also the quality of what was available in Swift's time. The histories of units from World War II continued to grow. The size of the student body made it necessary to keep the Library open evenings for full utilization. The limitation of space, for both books and students, became a problem even after the Library expanded into the East Academic Building. Actually, the growing needs of the Library had been neglected. Upon self-examination it became obvious that some unfavorable comments by the visiting Accrediting Committee of the Middle States Association of Colleges were justified. Consultant Robert H. Haynes of the Harvard University Library found that the Academy was at the bottom of the list in comparison with other colleges on the amount of money spent for books. In 1946, 1947, and 1949 the average was $5,219 a year for books and periodicals. In 1948 the amount was even less. Haynes thought $15,000 should be the minimum amount. Some high school libraries were already spending as much. The subtle movement toward a new and spacious library had begun. A process of inevitability came with the growth of the Academy and the growth of the collections.

As soon as the Academy had an Archivist, a steady number of Library bulletins began to appear, such as *Cadet Life before the Mexican War* in 1945, and *The Educational Objectives of the U. S. Military Academy* in 1946. These bulletins currently number eighteen, covering not only historical subjects but also the liberal arts, military medicine, the social sciences, and orientalia. *West Point, A History of the United States Military Academy*, the first complete treatment of the subject, was published by Dr. Forman in 1950. Dr. Forman was Archivist, historian and, finally, U. S. M. A. Librarian in 1958. The process of formally integrating the Library into the academic program slowly developed. If a library plays

Dr. Sidney Forman, Librarian from 1958 to 1962.

The demolition of the 1841 Library in 1962.

A close view of the destruction of the 1841 Library. Thayer Hall and the Hudson River are in the background.

no part in an academic program, it does not matter how many students are added to the student body. However, now the Library had to be taken seriously, with the broadening of the academic program to include more emphasis on liberal arts, the sending of more instructors to graduate schools, the growing limitations of the parochial departmental libraries, the increase in visiting professors, and the changing concept of textbook teaching. The Librarian became a member of the Superintendent's Staff, the first civilian so assigned. Now the Library's size and the imminent expansion of the Corps from 2,529 to 4,417 were inextricably and significantly related. The need for more space became critical. Several options were considered by various boards and committees. The most difficult obstacle to overcome was the warm regard held by all living graduates for the solemn dignity and richness of the standing Library. To destroy it seemed an abomination, yet the constraints of building areas and the absence of an organized resistance finally led to its demolition. A Library equal in square foot area to that of the recently completed Air Force Academy Library was planned, developed, and built on the site of the standing Library of 1841. Dr. Forman, after assisting in the architectural and furnishing plans for the new Library, took a position as Librarian at Columbia Teachers' College.

The new building will fulfill its role in promoting our proved concept of developing the 'whole man' in our graduate, a man prepared to meet the most exacting challenge of our times: the struggle for the minds of men.

Major General James B. Lampert, Superintendent, *Address* **at Dedication Ceremony, 1964**

The frame of the present Library in January, 1963.

Today's Library

Egon A. Weiss, Librarian from 1962 to the present.

Egon A. Weiss, having served as Associate Librarian for four years, became Librarian at the Academy on September 2, 1962, under the most difficult circumstances. The old Library had to be vacated, temporary facilities developed in the Mathematics Examination Room of Thayer Hall, and the move completed to the new building. The work began in 1962 and was finished with the dedication of the new Library on November 13, 1964. The Library Staff of about twenty-seven entered a new world—not only a new building, but a new world of modern, technical librarianship. The changes were quite radical because expansion of facilities and expansion of demand on library services came at the same time. The old Library could seat only eight percent of the Corps; the new Library could seat over twenty percent. Now library hours were extended to accommodate new academic requirements. Library support became the strong right arm of the academic program and necessitated the presence of trained, professional personnel to assist the cadets and faculty. Weiss began the gradual upgrading and enlargement of the Library Staff. His aim was to find or develop people who not only had library science degrees, but also had other subject background degrees. The best evidence of his success can be seen by the careers of those who worked under Mr. Weiss and moved on to higher positions. One is currently interconnecting and establishing the automation of

The Library today. The only adornment on the building is the 18-foot-high figure of Pallas Athena at the top of the tower. Lee Laurie, the sculptor, completed the work just before his death.

The Reference Room of the Library, probably the most utilized section, has a portrait of General Ulysses S. Grant on one wall, and General Robert E. Lee on the opposite wall.

all Army and Air Force libraries in Europe; one was Head Librarian of Eisenhower College and is now Head of Collection Development at Rochester Institute of Technology; one is Chief of Reference Branch, National Agricultural Library; one is Director of the National Defense Library; one became Project Manager with GEAC and is now automating the resources of the Smithsonian; one is head of the Valparaiso University Library in Indiana; one is Chief Librarian at the University of California at San Diego and has recently accepted the position of Director of Libraries at Yale University. Each of these professional librarians made notable contributions to the Academy Library in upgrading collections, cataloguing, designing library aids and bibliographies, and publishing bulletins. The current Library Staff is equaling, if not exceeding, their accomplishments.

Weiss has made every effort to augment the Library's special collections. True scholarship, he believes, must explore available primary sources—manuscripts and documents—and rare books. Advanced study and research have already become bulwarks of the academic program. The Library's strength has always been the support of the curriculum and collections in the history of military art, military technology, and the history of the United States Army, with emphasis on West Point and the Revolutionary War in the Hudson Hghlands. Alumni, as well as generous friends and bibliophiles, have contributed to the continuing growth and preservation of these unique resources with renewed vigor over the last quarter century. The establishment of "Friends of the West Point Library" in 1982 has already assisted the Library's growth of excellence.

In 1926, when Edward Aloysius Everts applied for the position of Librarian, he was Secretary of a lumber company—his main qualification for Librarian was his love of books. He wrote to the

The Periodical Room receives hundreds of magazines of general interest and diversion in addition to the scholarly serials.

View of the current newspaper holdings in the Library. Cadets are able to follow news in all parts of the United States and the world.

Adjutant General, "I really believe, Colonel, that I could fill the position, especially since there is a trained assistant to help in such library procedure as I would have to learn at first." He was, of course, appointed Librarian. Today's Library is light years away from the Library of 1926, not only in time, but also in advanced library technology. As recently as the early 1960's the Library depended on the generosity of Cornell, Columbia, Harvard, Duke, and Yale for cooperative library borrowings. However, the establishment of the Ramapo-Catskill and Mid-Hudson Library Systems, the 3R's (Reference, Research, Resources) System with its Southeastern Bibliographic Center, and the vast New York State Interlibrary Loan Network immediately expanded the available resources of the Academy Library. The limitations of the Dewey Decimal System led Weiss to begin the conversion of the entire Library to the Library of Congress Catalogue System, with no small objections from some of the older members of the staff. The conversion was almost immediately justified by the installation of the compatible resources of the OCLC (Online Computer Library Center) in 1973. This formidable reclassification project, accompanied by critically-needed recataloguing, was dramatically accelerated by the use of computer terminals. Thus, a sizeable portion of the collection was already in machine-readable format when computerization of the Library's holdings began in 1981. This public access circulation system does not yet contain the entire catalogue, nor has it reached its full potential in cross-referencing; however, it is very likely that it will one day provide access from any point on the Post. Today the OCLC contains over 10,600,000 bibliographic records, to which 23,000 are added weekly. The Academy's DIALOG tie joins 50,000 other using agencies to access 100,000,000 items. The internal GEAC facility, which provides electronic access to the catalogue, presently contains 250,000 of the Library's holdings. The use and maintenance of these devices make extensive demands on the technicians and their supervisors.

The Library, like any college or university library, lends itself to many uses. It has a teaching function in that the staff provides bibliographical instruction, interpretive services, mediation, information dissemination, and copy services. This instruction covers not only retrieval but evaluation as well. The Library has been used for chamber music concerts, art exhibits, conferences, SCUSA meetings, classes, and even small graduation ceremonies. The Librarian is assisted by a Library Committee of the Academic Board, of which he is a member, and which has cadet representation. Most likely, the Library will continue to grow and become more integrated in the teaching process. The individualization in the academic program must, of its nature, lead the student to the Library. Today, no one can become a Rhodes Scholar, or even an educated person, without spending time in the Library. Meanwhile, the Library itself, no matter how automated, will make higher demands on the Librarian and his Staff as the expansion in the growth of knowledge continues.